TOTAL
SOCCER

BY TODD KORTEMEIER

SportsZone

An Imprint of Abdo Publishing
www.abdopublishing.com

abdopublishing.com

Published by Abdo Publishing, a division of ABDO, PO Box 398166, Minneapolis, Minnesota 55439. Copyright © 2017 by Abdo Consulting Group, Inc. International copyrights reserved in all countries. No part of this book may be reproduced in any form without written permission from the publisher. SportsZone™ is a trademark and logo of Abdo Publishing.

Printed in the United States of America, North Mankato, Minnesota
092016
012017

Cover Photos: Jack Abuin/Cal Sport Media/AP Images, foreground; Volodymyr Burdiak/ Shutterstock Images, background
Interior Photos: Volodymyr Burdiak/Shutterstock Images, 1; Alex Grimm/AP Images, 4–5; Harro Schweizer/picture-alliance/dpa/AP Images, 6; Masanori Genko/Yomiuri Shimbun/ AP Images, 8; Christopher Futcher/iStockphoto, 10–11; EMPICS/EMPPL EMPICS Sports Photo Agency/Press Association/AP Images, 12, 15; Archive/Agência Estado/AP Images, 16–17; Manu Fernandez/AP Images, 19; Fotosports International/Newscom, 20; Michael Caulfield/AP Images, 22–23; Petr David Josek/AP Images, 24; Darryl Dyck/The Canadian Press/AP Images, 26–27; Bob Thomas/iStockphoto, 29; iStockphoto, 30–31; Mikkel William/iStockphoto, 32; Red Line Editorial, 34–35; Jefferson Bernardes/Shutterstock Images, 37; Yuri Turkov/Shutterstock Images, 38–39; Celso Diniz/Shutterstock Images, 40; Philipp Schmidli/Getty Images, 42–43; Phillip Willcocks/Shutterstock Images, 44; Shutterstock Images, 46–47, 48; Dmytro Larin/Shutterstock Images, 50–51; Scott Winters/ Icon Sportswire, 53; JMP/Rex Features/AP Images, 54–55; Andres Kudacki/AP Images, 56; Jamie Francis/The Oregonian/AP Images, 58–59; PA Wire URN:22881985/Press Association/AP Images, 61

Editor: Patrick Donnelly
Series Designer: Jake Nordby

Publisher's Cataloging-in-Publication Data

Names: Kortemeier, Todd, author.
Title: Total soccer / by Todd Kortemeier.
Description: Minneapolis, MN : Abdo Publishing, 2017. | Series: Total sports |
    Includes bibliographical references and index.
Identifiers: LCCN 2016945671 | ISBN 9781680785074 (lib. bdg.) | ISBN
    9781680798357 (ebook)
Subjects: LCSH: Soccer--Juvenile literature.
Classification: DDC 796.334--dc23
LC record available at http://lccn.loc.gov/2016945671

CONTENTS

THE WORLD CUP

Soccer fans around the world dream of winning the World Cup. Every soccer-playing nation, no matter how small, has a chance to win it. From the tiny island of Tonga to five-time world champion Brazil, the World Cup is a truly global event.

The tournament is run by the Fédération Internationale de Football Association (FIFA). As of 2016, 209 countries were FIFA members. The World Cup is held every four years. One country plays host to the final 32 teams. The process of qualifying for the final tournament takes several years. Teams began qualifying for the

Germany captain Bastian Schweinsteiger holds the World Cup trophy aloft before a massive crowd at Berlin's Brandenburg Gate in 2014.

Coach Vittorio Pozzo, *back row, third from left*, and his players celebrate Italy's 1938 World Cup victory.

2018 World Cup in March 2015. As host, Russia automatically qualifies. The rest of the teams battle for spots. They play against other countries from their region of the world.

The 32-team finals take place over approximately one month. First, the teams are placed into eight groups of four. The teams in each group all play each other once. This is known as "pool play." The top two teams in each group advance to the next round. These 16 teams then square off in a single-elimination tournament, or the "knockout rounds."

Countries bid for the right to host the tournament. The first World Cup was held in Uruguay in 1930. Except for 1942 and 1946, it has been held every four years since. Eight different countries have won the World Cup. Brazil has been the most successful. It has won five world titles and has qualified for every tournament.

Germany and Italy nearly match Brazil's success. They each have four World Cup wins. Germany has the tournament's all-time leading goal scorer.

WORLD CUP TROPHY

The first trophy awarded to the World Cup winner was called the Jules Rimet Trophy. It disappeared in 1966 and was later found buried under a tree. After Brazil won its third World Cup, rules said it got to keep the trophy. But in 1983, the cup was stolen in Rio de Janeiro. It was never found. The current World Cup trophy is made of 18-karat gold, stands 14 inches (36 cm) high, and weighs more than 13 pounds (6 kg).

8

Miroslav Klose scored two goals at the 2014 World Cup in Brazil, giving him 16 in his World Cup career. Klose helped Germany win its fourth title.

The World Cup is the most-watched sporting event on the planet. The 2014 tournament had an in-home television audience of 3.2 billion people. More than 1 billion watched the final match alone.

The FIFA Women's World Cup has taken place every four years since 1991. In that time, the United States has been on top of the women's soccer world. Team USA has won three World Cup titles, including the first one in China in 1991.

More than 90,000 fans packed the Rose Bowl to watch the United States defeat China in the 1999 Women's World Cup final.

Miroslav Klose scores his 16th career World Cup goal in Germany's semifinal victory over Brazil in 2014.

2

THE BEAUTIFUL GAME

One of the reasons soccer is the world's most popular sport is its simplicity. It comes down to kicking a ball into a goal. It is a sport that anyone can play and understand. Its roots can be traced back approximately 2,000 years.

The ancient Chinese people played a game called *Tsu' Chu*. They used a ball made of leather stuffed with hair and feathers. The goal was only 12 to 15 inches (30 to 38 cm) wide and made of bamboo. Approximately 500 years later, the Japanese played a game called *Kemari*. The object

Soccer is a simple game that can be enjoyed by people of all ages.

The Great Britain national soccer team won the Olympic gold medal in 1908.

of this game was to keep the ball in the air. Players would stand in a circle and pass the ball to each other.

Modern soccer dates back to the 1860s. That is when soccer separated from other ball sports such as rugby. The games were all similar up to that point. Rules were not well established. Some sports involved carrying and passing the ball, while others did not.

In 1863 men in Cambridge, England, got together to lay down rules for their version of the game. Their rules resembled what eventually became the modern version of soccer. However, carrying the ball was still allowed until 1869. This first meeting marked the beginning of England's Football Association (FA). The FA was one of the world's first sports leagues.

The first international soccer match took place in 1872. It was between England and Scotland. Great Britain was really where the modern game of

THE FA CUP

The oldest ongoing sports competition is England's FA Cup. As more teams started joining the FA, they decided to start a tournament to see which was best. Only 15 teams competed for the first FA Cup in 1871–72. But the tournament quickly became popular. Approximately 200,000 fans were on hand for the 1923 final at London's Wembley Stadium. Every team that belongs to the FA can enter the tournament. More than 700 teams now take part in the FA Cup every season.

soccer took off. From there its popularity spread to the rest of Europe and to South America. Argentina was the first South American country to form a soccer association in 1893.

FIFA formed in 1904 with seven members. By 1930, when the first World Cup was held, 41 countries were members of FIFA. Today the most-watched sports league is England's Premier League. Almost 5 billion people tune in to Premier League action each season. Other popular leagues exist throughout Europe as well. Germany's Bundesliga, Spain's La Liga, and Italy's Serie A all feature top players from around the world.

Through 2016 Manchester United and Arsenal were tied for the most FA Cup championships with 12 titles apiece.

In 1883 Blackburn Olympic became the first club from northern England to win the FA Cup.

¡GOLAZO!

The ball bends and twists its way toward the goal. The crowd rises in anticipation. With a bulge of the net, the fans explode in jubilation. Nothing brings people to their feet like an incredible goal. It's no wonder some of the most popular soccer players in history are goal scorers.

Many people consider Pelé to be the best soccer player ever. The Brazilian scored 767 goals in his career, which began in 1956. He won three World Cups and helped increase soccer's profile around the world. FIFA named Pelé the greatest player of the twentieth century.

Pelé fights off a defender from Romania during a 1970 World Cup game.

Germany's Gerd Müller scored 735 goals in his career. He scored nearly one goal per game during his time with German team Bayern Munich. Müller led the German league in goals seven times. He was named the best player in Europe in 1970.

Cristiano Ronaldo of Portugal and Real Madrid scored his 500th goal in 2015. Argentinian Lionel Messi got his 500th in 2016 at the age of 28. Messi also plays for FC Barcelona. The two rivals have waged many famous battles in their Spanish professional league.

These great players have scored their share of amazing goals. In 1959 Pelé dribbled the ball over three defenders before he headed it into the net.

GOAL-LINE TECH

In soccer the ball needs to completely cross the goal line to count as a goal. It can be hard for a referee to see. FIFA devised a review system after a number of high-profile disputed goals, including one at the 2010 World Cup. Goal-line technology made its first appearance in 2012. It was also used at the 2014 World Cup. Cameras from several different angles track the ball. The cameras can show whether it fully crossed the line for a goal or stayed out.

In Spanish-speaking countries, an amazing goal such as that is known as a *golazo*.

For athleticism, it doesn't get much better than the bicycle kick. A player does a reverse somersault and kicks the ball out of the air above his or her head. Zlatan Ibrahimovic of Sweden scored one of these against England in 2012 from more than 20 yards (18 m) away.

Of course, some of the most memorable goals have come in the World Cup. Argentina's Diego Maradona scored two in one half against England in a 1986 quarterfinal. The first was controversial. The replay showed the ball went off Maradona's hand. He later said "the hand of God" guided it into the net. The second goal was one of the best of all time. Maradona dribbled past five England defenders on a half-field run and scored the game-winner.

In 2012 Messi scored a record 91 goals in international and club play. Müller held the old record of 85.

Diego Maradona, *left*, scores his infamous "hand of God" goal against England keeper Peter Shilton in 1986.

4 WOMEN IN SOCCER

Approximately 30 million women and girls around the world play soccer. The first-ever Women's World Cup was held in 1991, 61 years after the first men's edition. But women's soccer is not new. Women have been playing it as long as men have.

As early as 1869, magazines showed women playing soccer. More than 120 women's matches were played in England and Scotland in the 1880s and 90s. They shared stadiums with men's teams and drew crowds of 10,000 fans. During World War I (1914–1918), many men were away fighting.

Members of Team USA celebrate after defeating China in the 1999 Women's World Cup final.

Marta blasts a penalty kick against the United States during the 2011 Women's World Cup.

Women's teams got the spotlight and often played in front of huge crowds.

The popularity of women's soccer declined after the war. Women were even banned by the FA from playing in men's stadiums until 1969. By then the sport was just beginning to take off in the United States. Federal legislation created more sports opportunities for girls. This helped the United States develop a strong national team.

In 2015 more than 400 million people watched the Women's World Cup. It was held in Canada. The United States has consistently been the top team in women's soccer. But Brazil's Marta is perhaps the best player ever. She is always a threat to score when the ball is on her foot. Marta won the World Player of the Year award five years in a row (2006–10).

PEAK OF WOMEN'S PRO SOCCER

In 1917 the Dick, Kerr and Company factory staged a soccer game. One team was male employees, the other female. The women beat the men. The factory bosses thought they might have the makings of a successful team. Dick, Kerr Ladies FC was formed and began play later that year. In 1920 they drew 53,000 fans to watch them play in Liverpool, England. DK Ladies won 758 matches and lost only 24 before they disbanded in 1965.

5

MISCONDUCT

The game of soccer is simple, but it has plenty of rules. FIFA publishes its "Laws of the Game" each year. The list consists of 17 rules. It describes everything from the field of play to the equipment players wear.

Every soccer game has a referee. It's his or her job to enforce the rules. The referee also must punish players whenever necessary. Sometimes players commit fouls. Usually a foul occurs when a player makes too much contact with another player. The team fouled gets to restart with a free kick from where the foul occurred.

If an attacking player is fouled near the net, the referee can call for a penalty kick.

THE INSPIRATION BEHIND CARDS

Referee Ken Aston knew that soccer matches could get out of hand. The Englishman refereed a tense match between Chile and Italy in the 1962 World Cup. Aston had to send off two Italian players in a match filled with fights. In the confusion, it wasn't clear who was sent off. Aston knew there had to be a clearer way to discipline players. While stopped at a traffic signal, the yellow and red lights gave him the inspiration. The cards made their debut at the 1970 World Cup. They have been used ever since.

The referee may award a penalty kick if an attacking player is fouled in the 18-yard (16.5-m) box around the keeper. In that event, a player from the attacking team takes a kick from a spot 12 yards (11 m) in front of the goal.

The punishment is more serious if the referee judges that a foul was intentional. A player is shown a yellow card for a first offense. That is considered a warning. If a player gets two yellow cards in a match, he or she is ejected. In some competitions, the player may miss the next match as well.

A player can also get immediately ejected. In this case,

A soccer player who is shown a red card is ejected from the game.

the referee shows the player a red card. Red cards are issued for very serious or violent fouls. Players who get a red card cannot be replaced. Their teams must play short-handed for the rest of the game.

6 EQUIPMENT

It would be impossible to play a soccer game without a ball. Over the years the ball has changed. At one time a pig's bladder inflated with air was used as a ball. In the 1830s, a vulcanized rubber center with a leather shell became the standard. As a result, the ball took on a rounder shape. The FA defined the circumference of the ball as 27 to 28 inches (69 to 71 cm) in 1872. That measurement has not changed since.

With the rise of the FA, sporting goods companies started making soccer balls in big numbers. The balls were leather and stitched

Shinguards, cleats, and a ball are among the most basic equipment every player should have.

The goalie wears gloves and a jersey that's a color different from his or her teammates' jerseys.

together like American footballs. These balls were much heavier than those used today. Balls without stitching appeared in the 1950s. By the 1980s balls were being made with synthetic leather. This made them much lighter.

Players don't wear much equipment in soccer. There's a jersey and shorts, plus a pair of cleats. Cleats are shoes with metal or plastic studs on the bottom. Players also wear pads over their shins called shinguards. These protect the shins from the cleats of opponents.

As the only player who can use his or her hands, the goalkeeper can wear gloves. The keeper's jersey also must be a color that's different from what the rest of the team wears. This is so the referee can easily spot the keeper in a crowd of players.

HEADGEAR IN SOCCER

Soccer players rarely wear head protection, despite frequently hitting the ball with their heads. One exception is Czech Republic goalkeeper Petr Cech. He has worn a specially designed helmet since 2006, when he fractured his skull in a collision with another player while playing for Chelsea in the English Premier League. He missed three months of action after emergency surgery. Cech returned in 2007 and has played with his helmet ever since.

7 POSITIONS AND FORMATIONS

Soccer positions aren't set in stone. A forward is on the field to score goals. But sometimes forwards find themselves playing defense. However, in general, teams place their players in specific formations. These formations define how a team attacks and defends.

One of the most common formations is the 4–4–2. That means there are four defenders, four midfielders, and two forwards. The goalkeeper is not included in the count. Each of those general groups is broken down into specific positions. Defenders in the center of the field are called

K - Keeper
D - Defender
M - Midfielder
F - Forward

In this diagram, the blue team is playing in a 4–4–2 formation, while the red team is set up in a 4–5–1.

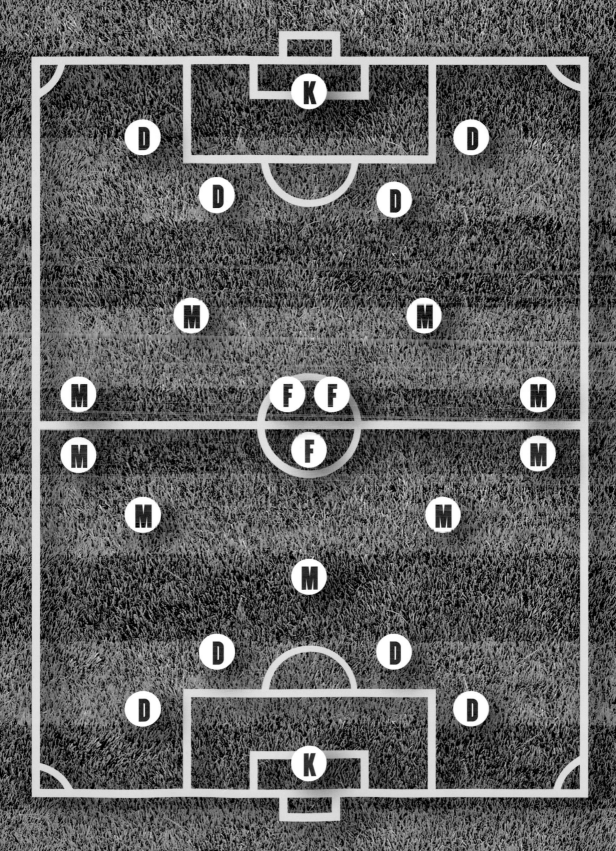

SQUAD NUMBERS

Many great soccer players wear No. 10 on their jerseys. Lionel Messi, Neymar, and Wayne Rooney are some of the world's best goal scorers. They all wear No. 10. It has become a tradition. Soccer players once had their numbers assigned them based on formation. The goalkeeper got No. 1. Then the defenders, midfielders, and forwards were assigned higher numbers in that order. So a team's best scorer—one of the forwards—often ended up with No. 10.

center backs. Players on the outside are left or right backs. Some midfielders play more on defense. Some hold the ball and attack. Forwards receive the ball to score goals.

Teams try to pick a formation that plays to their strengths. The 4–4–2 formation is good for teams with strong midfielders. An attacking team may want an extra forward or two. They might start with a 4–3–3 or 4–2–4. Teams try to avoid changing their formation often. Consistent practice with a certain formation allows players to anticipate where their teammates should be without looking for them.

Brazil's Neymar is one of many great scorers to wear No. 10.

LEGENDARY GROUNDS

Soccer stadiums are often rather basic. They're made to get fans in, let them watch the match, and get them out. But a soccer stadium comes alive once the fans are inside. Fans chant and sing. Players make history on the field. Some stadiums create memories to last a lifetime.

For English fans, it doesn't get better than Wembley Stadium in London. It's the home of the English national team and the FA Cup Final. It opened in 1923. But it was totally renovated in 2007. The new stadium is state of the art. It now plays host to a new generation of heroes.

Wembley Stadium is the center of English soccer.

The Maracana in Rio de Janeiro underwent renovations before hosing the 2014 World Cup and 2016 Olympic Games.

Soccer is a national passion in Brazil. The Maracana is the center of that passion. It is located in Rio de Janeiro. The Maracana hosted nearly 200,000 fans for the 1950 World Cup final. And it has been the site of many of Brazil's greatest soccer moments. But that 1950 final was one of its worst. Brazil lost the World Cup that day to Uruguay.

Argentina is another South American soccer power. Boca Juniors play at La Bombonera in the capital of Buenos Aires. Passionate Boca fans make this stadium one of the toughest places to play in the world. The field actually shakes with the jumping and cheering of the fans.

Spain's Barcelona is another famous club. And it has one of the biggest stadiums. Camp Nou holds nearly 100,000 fans. Fans come decked out in the club's blue and red colors to cheer on Lionel Messi and his teammates.

FAMOUS WORLD CUP STADIUMS

Only three stadiums have hosted the World Cup final twice. They are Brazil's Maracana, Germany's Olympiastadion, and Mexico's Estadio Azteca. The first-ever indoor World Cup match was held at the Silverdome in Pontiac, Michigan, in 1994. That 1994 World Cup holds the all-time record for average attendance. An average of 68,991 fans attended.

9

SOCCER vs. FOOTBALL

In the United States, the word *football* means the sport with helmets and touchdowns. In most other countries *football* means soccer. It's even in FIFA's name. That version of football is the most popular sport in most of the world. American football doesn't have much of a following outside the United States.

Although Americans call it *soccer*, the word isn't an American invention. It is a shortening of *association football*. The term was coined in England. In the early 1900s, it was fashionable

FIFA, headquartered in Zurich, Switzerland, is soccer's international governing body.

Arsenal has a cannon in its logo to represent its team nickname.

to shorten words. Rugby was known as "rugger." Likewise, association football became "soccer."

Both "football" and "soccer" were used to refer to the sport in England until the 1980s. But as the game became more popular in the United States, use of the term "soccer" declined in England. In the United States, there was a reverse effect. US Soccer was founded in 1913 as the US Football Association. It didn't adopt its current name until 1974.

The United States isn't the only country where people call the sport *soccer*. Australia has its own version of football that is different from soccer and American football. So in Australia, the sport with the round ball is called *soccer*.

Most other countries use "football," but it goes by a few other names. In Italy, the game is often called *calcio*. That word comes from a Latin term meaning "heel" or "kick."

PREMIER LEAGUE NICKNAMES

Most sports teams in the United States have nicknames—Yankees, Vikings, Warriors, etc. Premier League soccer teams have nicknames too. But they usually aren't decided by the team itself. These nicknames usually have a historical basis. Or they come from the fans. Arsenal is known as the "Gunners." One of the club's founders worked at a weapons factory. Manchester United became the "Red Devils" because of its red uniforms.

10 OTHER KINDS OF SOCCER

You don't need 22 players and a huge space to play soccer. Over the years, alternative versions of the game have grown popular. Some of these spinoffs have developed into organized, international competitions.

Futsal dates back to Uruguay in 1930. The game was designed to be played indoors with just five players per team. A futsal court is a hard surface that is a little larger than a basketball court. The ball is a little smaller and not as bouncy. Halves last 20 minutes instead of 45. FIFA holds a Futsal World Cup every four years.

Futsal is played indoors on a hard court.

Another indoor game is simply called indoor soccer. It is played in arenas using the boards of a hockey rink. This makes for a very different game. The ball rarely goes out of bounds. Players can use the boards to pass. There is no offside rule. Indoor soccer also moves fast and features a lot of scoring.

Beach soccer is just what it sounds like. Players in this game contend with an uneven sand surface. Beach soccer has five players per side. Players don't need cleats. They play in bare feet. Beach soccer players can make crazy midair kicks because they can land on a soft surface.

PELADA

Kids in Brazil love to play soccer. They might not have a field or the right equipment. But they will play anywhere, with anything that passes for a ball. They call the game *pelada*. Players line up to play in any fenced-in area they can find Sometimes the ball is made out of plastic bags or socks—whatever it takes to have a game. Many players on the Brazil national teams grew up playing this way. Pelada helps kids learn how to properly touch and control the ball.

Players can try acrobatic moves in beach soccer because the playing surface is so forgiving.

FRENZIED FANS

Turn on any soccer match from around the world. You're likely to hear singing, chanting, and maybe even some drumming. You'll see waving flags, signs, and scarves. Soccer fans are passionate.

Part of it is just love of the sport. But soccer fans identify closely with their teams. In the case of a national team, it's country pride. For professional soccer, it's the town or neighborhood a club represents. Fans in the stands take that seriously. It's not just the players playing. It's all of them together.

Italy fans show their support at the 2012 European Championship.

GLOBETROTTING FANS

The countries that send the most fans to the World Cup are usually those whose teams have the best chance of winning. At the 2014 World Cup in Brazil, locals bought the most tickets. But the United States, a country not known for its soccer passion was second. Almost 200,000 Americans bought World Cup tickets, far ahead of third-place Argentina with 61,000. It's a sign of soccer's rising popularity in the United States.

Soccer fans love chants and songs. There's a song for any purpose. Some celebrate certain players. Some make fun of the other team. Songs are often based on pop songs. One of the most common has only one word. "*Olé, Olé, Olé*" can be heard at many stadiums, even in places where Spanish isn't spoken.

Soccer fans are known for traveling. No matter where the World Cup is played, every country has fans who will do what it takes to be there. Some of the biggest clubs have fans all over the world as well.

A young girl cheers for Team USA at the 2016 Olympics.

12 DERBIES

Every match is important to fans. But some are bigger than others. Every soccer team has at least one opponent that fans love to hate. A rivalry game in soccer is called a derby. Some derbies date back more than 100 years. They are battles for both players and fans.

A lot of derbies take place between teams that play their home games near each other. London teams Tottenham Hotspur and Arsenal have played each other since 1887. But their rivalry didn't really begin until Arsenal moved in next door to Tottenham in 1913. The teams now play

Yaya Toure, *right*, leads a Manchester City charge against Manchester United defender Chris Smalling.

approximately 4 miles (6.4 km) apart in north London. The North London Derby is one of the most intense rivalries in English soccer.

In Northwest England, two clubs battle to rule Manchester. Both share the city's name—Manchester City and Manchester United. The two have played each other since 1881. United has usually come out on top. But with City's Premier League championships in 2012 and 2014, the Manchester Derby has become much more heated.

Some rivalries are explosive. Turkey's Fenerbaçhe and Galatasaray have been playing since 1909. Supporters of each team frequently light up the stadium with flares and torches. The smoke and lights make for a very intimidating environment.

Some rivalries endure no matter what The Portland Timbers and Seattle Sounders are two of the biggest rivals in Major League Soccer (MLS), the top league in the United States. Their rivalry dates back to 1975. But the two teams have only been in MLS since 2011. Their mutual dislike has survived through 40 years and four different leagues. Four of their matchups at Seattle are on the list of the top 10 biggest crowds in MLS history.

EL CLÁSICO

One of the world's most-watched rivalries comes from Spain. Its two biggest cities have two of the world's most famous soccer teams. When Barcelona and Real Madrid get together, it's called *El Clásico*—the classic. Approximately 500 million people watch each year.

13
STAR-SPANGLED
SOCCER

To the rest of the world, the United States was an odd choice to host the 1994 World Cup. There was no pro outdoor soccer league in the country when the game was awarded in 1988. FIFA insisted that the United States needed to start a league to host the World Cup.

The World Cup was a big success. It set records for attendance. Clearly many Americans liked soccer. Major League Soccer (MLS) kicked off in 1996 with 10 teams. But the league didn't have many established stars. And teams played in stadiums designed for American football.

The Timbers Army drums up support for the Portland Timbers.

MLS grew steadily in popularity from those humble beginnings. By 2016 the league had 20 teams, with eight more planned. Stars from the US men's national team and international clubs had signed on with MLS teams.

The world took notice when English superstar David Beckham joined the Los Angeles Galaxy in 2007. But Beckham was far from the only big-name European player to join an MLS team. Steven Gerrard also signed with the Galaxy in 2015. In his previous season with Liverpool in the English Premier League, he was the team captain and leading goal scorer. Two-time African Player of the Year Didier Drogba signed with the Montreal Impact in 2015.

MLS is divided into Eastern and Western Conferences, each with 10 teams. The top six

THE NASL

MLS followed in the footsteps of the North American Soccer League (NASL). That league operated from 1968 to 1984. In the 1970s, the NASL was able to attract major soccer stars from around the world. Legends such as Pelé and Franz Beckenbauer played in front of huge crowds with the New York Cosmos.

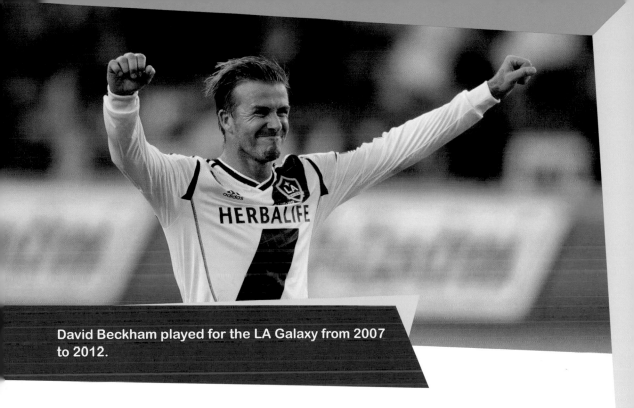

from each conference make the playoffs. The last two teams remaining play for the MLS Cup.

MLS has similar attendance to some of the best leagues in the world. With an average crowd of more than 21,000, more fans attend MLS matches than the top leagues in France or the Netherlands. The Seattle Sounders lead MLS with an average of more than 44,000 fans per game.

Soccer is not the most popular sport in the United States. But there's no doubt it has a place in the hearts of many American sports fans.

GLOSSARY

banned
Prevented from happening for a period of time.

controversial
A result that is subject to interpretation or debate.

debut
First appearance.

derby
A game between two heated rivals.

dribble
In soccer, the touches on the ball by a player as it is taken up the field.

offside
In soccer, a rules violation in which an offensive player is behind the last defender when the ball is played.

rival
An opponent with whom a player or team has a fierce and ongoing competition.

single-elimination
A tournament in which one loss eliminates a team from competing.

FOR MORE INFORMATION

Books

Marthaler, Jon. *Soccer Trivia*. Minneapolis, MN: Abdo Publishing, 2016.

Mills, Andrea. *The Soccer Book*. Buffalo, NY: Firefly Books, 2016.

Trusdell, Brian, *Soccer Record Breakers*. Minneapolis, MN: Abdo Publishing, 2015.

Websites

To learn more about soccer, visit **booklinks.abdopublishing.com**. These links are routinely monitored and updated to provide the most current information available.

INDEX

ABOUT THE AUTHOR

Todd Kortemeier studied journalism and English at the University of Minnesota and has authored dozens of books for young people, primarily on sports topics. He lives in Minneapolis, Minnesota, with his wife.